CARESS/ACHE

BY SUZIE MILLER

CURRENCY PRESS
SYDNEY

GRIFFIN THEATRE COMPANY

CURRENT THEATRE SERIES

First published in 2015
by Currency Press Pty Ltd,
Gadigal Land, Suite 310, 46-56 Kippax Street, Surry Hills NSW 2012 Australia
enquiries@currency.com.au; www.currency.com.au
in association with Griffin Theatre Company

Copyright: © Suzie Miller, 2014, 2015.

COPYING FOR EDUCATIONAL PURPOSES

The Australian *Copyright Act 1968* (Act) allows a maximum of one chapter or 10% of this book, whichever is the greater, to be copied by any educational institution for its educational purposes provided that that educational institution (or the body that administers it) has given a remuneration notice to Copyright Agency Limited (CAL) under the Act.

For details of the CAL licence for educational institutions contact CAL, Level 15/233 Castlereagh Street, Sydney, NSW, 2000; tel: within Australia 1800 066 844 toll free; outside Australia 61 2 9394 7600; fax: 61 2 9394 7601; email: info@copyright.com.au

COPYING FOR OTHER PURPOSES

Except as permitted under the Act, for example a fair dealing for the purposes of study, research, criticism or review, no part of this book may be reproduced, stored in a retrieval system, or transmitted in any form or by any means without prior written permission. All enquiries should be made to the publisher at the address above.

Any performance or public reading of *Caress / Ache* is forbidden unless a licence has been received from the author or the author's agent. The purchase of this book in no way gives the purchaser the right to perform the play in public, whether by means of a staged production or a reading. All applications for public performance should be addressed to HLA Management, hla@hlamgt.com.au .

No part of this book may be used or reproduced in any manner for the purpose of training artificial intelligence technologies or systems without the express written permission of the author and the publisher.

Cataloguing-in-publication data for this title is available from the National Library of Australia website: www.nla.gov.au

Typeset by Dean Nottle for Currency Press.
Front cover shows Ian Stenlake.
Cover photograph by Brett Boardman. Cover design by RE:.

Currency Press acknowledges the Traditional Owners of the Country on which we live and work. We pay our respects to all Aboriginal and Torres Strait Islander Elders, past and present.

Contents

CARESS / ACHE	1

Acknowledgement and thanks are due for the support and development provided by:

National Theatre Studio (London) for two weeks of fully supported development.

National Theatre Studio

Frantic Assembly London—Steven Hogget and Scott Graham—for script notes.

Caress / Ache was first produced by Griffin Theatre Company at the SBW Stables Theatre, Sydney, on 27 February 2015, with the following cast:

DR MARK ANDERS/ADAM	Ian Stenlake
SASKIA/LIBBY	Helen Christinson
AREZU/CATE	Sabryna Te'o
PETER/CAMERON	Gary Clementson
BELINDA/ALICE	Zoe Carides

Director, Anthony Skuse
Designer, Sophie Fletcher
Lighting Designer, Matthew Marshall
Sound Designer, Nate Edmondson

CHARACTERS

DR MARK ANDERS, paediatric cardio-thoracic surgeon, 30s/40s
SASKIA, female book editor, 20/30s
CAMERON, male poet, 20/30s
AREZU, young woman, 20s
CATE, call centre worker, mother of Adam, 20/30s
BELINDA, call centre worker, 20/30s
PETER, young man, 20s
ALICE, Peter's mother, 40s
LIBBY, Mark's wife, 30/40s
ADAM, child played as an extra role by one of actors (male or female)
OPERATING THEATRE ASSISTANTS
AIRLINE ATTENDANTS
SECURITY GUARDS

Ages are guides only. The characters should be of any ethnicity and cast on a completely colour-blind basis noting also that Arezu must not be a Middle-Eastern stereotype.

The playwright consents to names being changed for characters if appropriate to actors' ethnicities.

If actors are doubling, here are some suggestions:

Actor 1: Mark
Actor 2: Peter/Cameron
Actor 3: Saskia/Libby or Saskia/Belinda
Actor 4: Arezu/Cate
Actor 5: Alice/Belinda or Alice/Libby
All actors play Operating Theatre Assistants, Airline Attendants, Airport Security Guards

IMPORTANT NOTES

Throughout the text:

- / indicates the point where the next line begins—be it a point where the next line overlaps the rest of the original line, or the point at the end of the original line where the following line begins immediately without a beat

- — indicates a thought that is truncated by the character stopping themselves from saying any more

- … indicates a trailing thought, not the truncated one

- [*UK version*:] text within is for the UK version of the same show

The play can be either a chamber piece or a large-scale piece.

All stage directions are suggestions only. Sometimes they are just raising possibilities—the director should feel free to ignore or incorporate.

This play went to press before the end of rehearsals and may differ from the play as performed.

SCENE 1

Can be spoken by any actor or surtitled:

> *'Human skin and tissues contain millions of sensory receptors. Without them, there would be no capacity for people to sense the touch of another.'*

Classical music and the sound of a heart monitoring machine beeping in time.

Otherwise all human sounds are absent.

The movement of people could mirror Scene 23 at the Airport.

DR MARK ANDERS, *white coat, white surgical mask hanging around his neck.*

There can be ASSISTANTS *on stage also in surgical gear.*

MARK *is operating.*

Aware of the music.

His action is fluid, smooth, coordinated, within control.

MARK: Inside every note.
　　Dancing.
　　Every silent moment.
　　Muscle
　　memory.
　　Purposeful,
　　unthinking,
　　stroking skin, prising tissue so new, so still of the womb
　　on the edges of
　　barely formed rib bones.
　　The score of the music reaches exact momentum.
　　Tender space between bars.

　　　Next lines can spoken by different OPERATING ASSISTANTS *or just the same one:*

OPERATING ASSISTANT: Paediatric.
OPERATING ASSISTANT: Cardio.
OPERATING ASSISTANT: Thoracic.

OPERATING ASSISTANT: Surgical procedure.
MARK: The beauty of this moment before the incision,
   the pace and tone.
   Intellect, practical perfection and intuition intertwined.
   Taut bare torso,
   clean canvas.

Do the lights start to beat (i.e. on and off) to the beat of the heart?

OPERATING ASSISTANT: One,
OPERATING ASSISTANT: two,
OPERATING ASSISTANT: three,
OPERATING ASSISTANT: the score begins.
MARK: And
   in my hand
   the scalpel.
   Slice
   through infant skin.
   Steel instruments
   moving in the cavity.
   My fingers probing like a sculptor, pressing down and lifting out
   the heart.
   And as I'm holding this—
   tiniest of organs
   in my fingertips,
   smaller than the stone of a plum.
   Pumping blood.
   Trusting, waiting, muscles contracting and releasing.
   It's strange warmth and folded self.
   Tributaries rushing desperately back toward its cavity.
   Then, only then do I feel, the majesty of life.
   —

   She says after surgery I fuck differently,
   with passion.
   My hands passing over her body.
   A rough gentleness.
   I'm holding the muscle in my hand.
   Drawing it together to repair what nature couldn't.
   I am in charge.

Holding life here in my hands.
—
—
But then—
The music

   Mood change.

It's
Out of
Time
With my
Fingers

   Do the lights start to falter? A slight change? A tremor?

I can't seem to hold the note.
This is a—
A—
A tremor, a current.
And—
And—
Before the machine sounds
I feel
something is wrong.
Placing the organ inside the cavity, preparing to close, this is the finale.
But my own heart is—
And there is this weird sickness in the base of my stomach.
This will not happen.
Eyes racing, searching.
Fingers massaging, gently pleading for control.
I want seamlessness, restitching with perfection.
Not this.
—
The muscle lies there,
still cradled in my hands,
rejoined to its place, and yet.
And yet.
This furious fighting, angry red pulsing is faltering.
Missing its moments.

Tension rises in the room but no-one—
No-one will speak.
I'm handed an instrument. Cold steel catching the light.
But I can't take it. I can't let go.
There's no reason for this.
No
reason.
My hands move methodically.
Calmly, kneading the muscle into its rhythm.
All of us entwined in this one tiny body.
The machine alerting us, timing us, timing me.
And suddenly there is no music only chaos.

> *Frantic, yet ordered.*
>
> *The energy and action matches the sense of frantic movement and time running out that is implicit in the scene.*

Electrical currents.
Beat, baby, beat, baby, beat, baby.
And when the alarm goes it is with the calmest of voices that I hear /
OPERATING ASSISTANT: We're losing her.
OPERATING ASSISTANT: Clamps.
OPERATING ASSISTANT: Timing.
MARK: Electric shocks rack through the warm body beneath us.
Tiny torso jumping.
More electricity.
Come on.
Count it down.
OPERATING ASSISTANT: One.
OPERATING ASSISTANT: Two.
OPERATING ASSISTANT: Three.
MARK: More.
Come on!
I dive in there, moving my fingers over the unresponsive piece of flesh.
Again.
Currents.
Again.

OPERATING ASSISTANT: Flatline.
MARK: Again.
OPERATING ASSISTANT: Flatline.
MARK: Again.
Again.
Again!

> *The sound of a flatline on a heart monitor.*
> MARK *stands bereft, unnecessary, lost, alone.*
> *Do the others leave him there?*
> *Or does the light source die right down so we only see his face?*

SCENE 2

Can be spoken by any actor or surtitled:

> 'Skin receptors respond immediately to touch, warmth and cold, but pain receptors are the most numerous.
> Every square centimetre of skin contains two receptors for cold, and one for warmth, but over two hundred receptors for pain.'

SASKIA *is in a frenzy tearing pages out of books, or out of manuscripts, and throwing them about the room.*

The room is a war zone.

Pages everywhere.

Tears and tears.

CAMERON *enters.*

CAMERON: What the fuck, Saskia—

> *He goes to grab her.*
> SASKIA *is poised, looking at him with a book of his in her hands, the guts about to be ripped out of it.*

That's my—
Put that down.
Have you lost? /

> SASKIA *slaps his face hard with the book as he touches her. He reels in horror.*

A look, a challenge from her.

You hit me?

SASKIA *picks up another book, reads the title.*

SASKIA: [*reading*] 'Eagles and Honesty—a collection of poetry'.
CAMERON: Saskia, you hit me.
SASKIA: Did it hurt?
CAMERON: Yes.

Beat.

Give me my book.
Now.

He goes to grab it but she pulls it away at the last moment.

SASKIA: [*accusing*] Tell me you didn't do it?
CAMERON: Do what?
SASKIA: Tell me.

She is poised with the book about to be ripped. He goes to grab it.

CAMERON: Don't you dare.

She dodges him.

SASKIA: Tell me you didn't do it? /
CAMERON: I don't know what you're fucking talking about.
SASKIA: Tell me, tell me now.
CAMERON: Tell you *what?!* /
SASKIA: Tell me you didn't sleep with her.

Silence—his face changes entirely.

An admission of guilt.

Say it!

Beat.

Tell me it isn't true.
Tell me you didn't fuck her.

Silence.

Jesus.

She rips the guts out of the book she is holding—his book.

He sits, despondent,
guilty,
wordless.

SCENE 3

Can be spoken by any actor or surtitled:

> *'Emotional response can be experienced as physical touch stimulating the sensory receptors for cold.*
>
> *When an emotional event is experienced through hearing and sight, the physical reactions can include goosebumps and shivers.'*

MARK *is on the phone somewhere.*

ALICE *is also on the phone—but somewhere else.*

Through the air a soft almost unbearable lament can be heard.

Is it possible that they could appear to be talking to each other at first in a discordant manner and then we realise that they are two separate conversations?

MARK *is practising a speech before dialling.*

MARK: It seemed appropriate that
I should speak with you…
I thought I would call and properly offer my— /

> ALICE *has been on hold for some time to a government department.*

ALICE: No, I've already been on hold for—
About twenty minutes, I don't—
Yes but—
No but—
Yes, no please don't put me—
Oh God. /

MARK: I wasn't properly provided with an opportunity to express— express— /

ALICE: Hello, I am calling about government entitlements I could—
No no no, not Social Services.
No, I've already spoken to them.
No not—

Hold sounds.

MARK: [*still practising*] I just wanted to call and offer /
ALICE: I don't—
 No please they put me through to you.
 It's for money to subsidise an airfare.
 No for me, I'm—
 An airfare.
 Of course I'm serious, it's—
 No, please listen first.
 Oh, okay then, but will they be the right— [person?] /

 Hold sounds.

 MARK *dials.*

MARK: Hello. It's—

 He coughs. /

ALICE: Hello, I need—
 Oh hello, 'Luke'—
 I need to…
 Yes I'm fine thank you—
 I've been put through to you as the person who can help me /
MARK: Mrs Conway /
ALICE: No please please, don't do that. Look, what did you say your name was? /
MARK: I wanted to offer you my condolences /
ALICE: Luke.
 That's right.
 I've been on hold seven times already. /
MARK: Yes of course, I haven't said /
ALICE: I just want to speak to someone who can help me. /
MARK: It's Dr Anders, Mark Anders /
ALICE: Yes I know—
 Yes, I, I do understand—
 But, Luke, no-one seems to understand me. /
MARK: Yes I know I told you I would /
ALICE: If you would just let me explain— /
MARK: I just wanted to, to offer my condolences /

ALICE: No, no you can't transfer me. Please.
Can I just tell you, tell someone, please, Luke, you, can I just tell you— /
MARK: No, I wasn't trying to… /
ALICE: Really, you will? You'll— /
MARK: No, I'm so sorry I can't comment on that /
ALICE: Well, I was told that—Given the circumstances—My son.

Beat.

Peter. I was told that the government would pay for me to see him. /
MARK: No, no I just want to offer my sincerest /
ALICE: In Singapore /
MARK: It's a bad time, I should have waited /
ALICE: Yes.
Singapore /
MARK: Please, Mrs Conway, that isn't what happened /
ALICE: No of course this is not a joke—Someone from the Department of Foreign Affairs [*UK version:* Home Office]— /
MARK: Before the surgery I just thought /
ALICE: No
I don't understand,
anything. /
MARK: I don't know, I don't know. I know I said that /
ALICE: Yes, The Department of Foreign Affairs [*UK version:* Home Office]! /
MARK: I know, I said that but /
ALICE: No, I don't remember his— /
MARK: That's not true, No I, I, I— /
ALICE: No I— /
MARK: I just called to see if you're alright. /
ALICE: No, no I don't remember his bloody name. /
MARK: No of course you're not. I'm sorry /
ALICE: Luke. Luke?

Dead line sound. /

MARK: I shouldn't have called. I'm sorry I have, I have to go. /

Dead line sound.

Puts his phone down. His dead line merges with the dead line that is still flowing from ALICE.

SCENE 4

Can be spoken by any actor or surtitled:

'A baby is born familiar only with the touch and temperature of warm water.

The multiple somatic stimuli the baby experiences upon birth are all new and shocking.'

AREZU: The first time I see Uncle Mosa I've just turned seven,
I sneak out of bed,
watch Mum hugging him and speaking in a language I've never heard before.

Uncle Mosa is not my real uncle, but he talks to me more than the others,
he laughs at my TV shows,
asks me all about the rules of netball, about my friends,
my thoughts.

'Your name means Hope',
he tells me,
Arezu means hope,
a name from our old country,
'Yours is a name for the future'.

He brings me storybooks
filled with beautiful pictures
and when I am with him
I learn about places that are part of me
and I see things I've never seen before.

   Pause.

The next time he visits
I am nearly thirteen.
He tells me how much I have grown
that now I look like my mother.

One night he sits on my bed and recites poetry,

sounds and stories,

and he starts to tell me things

about feelings, real grown-up feelings.
And secrets that I know I can never tell my parents.

He is very still.

After my bedtime I hear him arguing with my mum and dad,
I have never heard them this upset.

I stay in my bed, put my earphones in, turn the volume up loud.

Then later on
it's the middle of the night,

Uncle Mosa shakes me and I wake up,

he has something for me.

A book wrapped up in rose-coloured tissue paper.

He says that poetry is part of my birthright
that I have a right to know.
He gives me the book.

Uncle Mosa says that one day we must all go back to Iran.
Take up the fight again and
put fear aside.

He speaks quickly now.

He says that things must change over there
we must bring equality back

and that one day he will take me,
show me what my parents won't,
let me see my homeland for myself.

And then, I can also be part of the fight.
Uncle Mosa says I have a purpose,
I am someone who will bring hope.
Just as my name says I will.

The next day he is gone.

He never comes back.

SCENE 5

Can be spoken by any actor or surtitled:
> *'The human tongue contains hundreds of minute receptors for taste. The tongue can therefore detect harmful products and avoid them— thus maintaining survival.'*

MARK *is at home with* LIBBY.
They set the table together.
Preparing for the evening meal.
She passes him cutlery and plates etc.
Everything appears normal as they almost dance around one another for up to a minute.
Then she stumbles and they nearly touch.
MARK *panics and visibly baulks.*
When their hands nearly touch, he backs away.
LIBBY *notices.*
He avoids any physical connection with her.
(Does she punish him once she realises that he won't go near her?
Does she flirt with him while she does the action? Trying to win him back, ultimately frustrated by him?)
Silence.

LIBBY: I went to the fish market this morning.
    My early meeting was cancelled
    So I just—
    Just left the office
    jumped in a cab,
    you know
    I'd never been there before!
MARK: —
LIBBY: All this activity.
MARK: —
LIBBY: People everywhere, and—

    There is a plate of oysters before them.

Oyster?

>   MARK *takes and eats the oysters.*

Steve tells me 'go to the north stall
and say, 'I don't want the oysters that've been frozen,
get them to delve into the buckets—right to the bottom where the fresh ones are'.
He said, 'Sound assertive' and they'll think you know.

MARK: —

LIBBY: And so I, I do.
I say, [*assertive*] 'I want the ones at the bottom'.
And they do, [*laughing*] they dig away
and Steve's right, these ones are the best.

MARK: —

LIBBY: Don't you think?
Mark, don't you think?

MARK: —

LIBBY: You know they're aphrodisiacs?
Makes you desire sex!

MARK: —

LIBBY: Which might be nice—

MARK: —

LIBBY: For us?

MARK: —

LIBBY: Anyway,
all the boys at college

MARK: —?

LIBBY: used to eat them with tequila.

>   MARK *is still eating the oysters.*

I never could though.
Eat them.
I'm fine now, but back then—

>   *She eats a whole oyster.*

I mean the thought of eating something while it was still— [beating]

>   MARK *stops eating, stops everything.*

You know.

Sliding down my throat. I don't—
> MARK *waits for her to explain.*
> *She has forced him to talk.*

MARK: What?
LIBBY: Well… you know
they're alive.
> MARK *immediately gags.*
> *Jumps up from the table.*
> LIBBY *tries to stroke his back.*

Mark?
> *Her arm is poison to him.*

For God's sake, Mark,
it's me,
Libby.
It's just my hand.
> *Beat.*

Mark, you have to let me in.
> MARK *gags.*
> *He spits the oyster up and leaves it sitting there between them.*
> *They look at it.*

SCENE 6

Can be spoken by any actor or surtitled:
> 'Some human receptors are enclosed in a capsule of connective tissue. They react to light touch and are located in the skin of lips, eyelids, external genitals and nipples.
>
> It is due to these special receptors that these areas of the body are particularly sensitive.'

BELINDA *and* CATE *are on running machines in work-out gear.*

Both have earphones strapped to their heads.

Both actors are wired for talking on the phone.

Both are walking/running throughout. (There could be running machines—or each actor could run with only one high heel on—a visual trick which makes it look like the actor is running on a machine.)

BELINDA: Gradient of four and pace of eight
  lets you work up a sweat.
  Which incidentally, helps!
CATE: —
BELINDA: With those numbers [*talking breathily*] I'm all breathy when I talk.
CATE: I might start at five.
BELINDA: Busiest time of the year.
  And they're always trying to get us to work extra,
  I'm like 'no way', I've got a life outside of work.
  So it's really great to have you.
CATE: —
BELINDA: This job though—
  When you think about it,
  we've got it all really.
  Young, earning the bucks and
  after a good go on this machine you've got a hot butt thrown in!
CATE: Yep yours looks pretty good.
BELINDA: Not that any of them get to see it!

   They laugh.

   CATE *is running on the machine.*

  You gotta time it. When you start you just walk. Then as you need to speed up.
  Are you—
  You're nervous!
CATE: [*she is a little*] No.
BELINDA: Boss wants me to listen in.
CATE: —
BELINDA: Just till you get the hang of it.
CATE: —
BELINDA: What? Don't look at me like that.
CATE: Sorry.
BELINDA: What?!

CATE: Nothing.

> BELINDA *laughs.*

BELINDA: I don't work here because I—
Well, just so you know
I'm not your trashy, cliché single mother trying to pay for her kid.

CATE: —

BELINDA: I'm saving. For a round the world trip. Get a buff bod in the meantime.

CATE: —

BELINDA: And you?
Saving?

CATE: For a trashy cliché!

BELINDA: Huh?

CATE: Poor single mother.

BELINDA: Oh.

CATE: Desperately trying to pay for her kid!

> BELINDA *laughs then stops.*

BELINDA: Oh fuck.
Jesus. Sorry.

> CATE *laughs, letting her off.*

CATE: No—
It's not—
He's a great kid.

> *A call comes in.*

BELINDA: It's yours!

> CATE *straightens her earphones.*
> *She is nervous.*

CATE: Hi there, Cate speaking.
Oh, hi Chris, how are you, baby?

> *She is adjusting the running machine to speed up a bit.*

> BELINDA *physically indicates for* CATE *to slow down.*

Yeah, I'm lying on my bed and I'm feeling really horny, I'm really wanting you. God, I want you so bad!

> BELINDA *starts running faster on the machine and gesticulates to* CATE *to slow down the talk.* BELINDA *mouths the words more slowly than* CATE *is saying them.*
>
> CATE *throws her a look after each line that queries whether she is on track, and takes feedback from* BELINDA, *who wildly gesticulates.*

I'm taking my panties off, Chris,
can you feel how wet I am?
Oh yes, sorry, okay then,
that's great, I can feel
your hand touching me.
Have you got your—

> *She is interrupted by something he says on the phone—he is moving her along in the story.*

Oh yes,
yes.
I can see you now, Chris,
oh, it's so big!
It's so huge.

> *She rolls her eyes at* BELINDA.
>
> BELINDA *is encouraging but tells her to slow down.*
>
> CATE *adjusts the machine but that is not what* BELINDA *means.*

I'm biting your shoulder. No. Okay. I'm lying back feeling you touching me. Oh sorry, yes I'm standing up—No—Yes sorry you're right, I'm straddling you and—Okay then: Oh yeah. Oh yeah. Oh Chris. Yes. Yes. Go baby. That's it. Yes you're riding inside me. Yes. Yes. *Yes!*
Sorry what was that?
Oh… you're welcome.
Is there—
Chris?
Hello?
   [*To* BELINDA] He hung up.
BELINDA: [*laughing*] Lesson number one:

Cate!—you don't use your
real name! /
CATE: Oh God, yes of course.
BELINDA: *And* even more importantly:
they pay by the minute so
you gotta string them out.
Or that kid of yours
he won't be getting much supporting!
CATE: God, he thanked me in
the middle of it!
BELINDA: String them out.
CATE: Then hung up!
BELINDA: Just go slow.

>   *Phone rings and* BELINDA *picks it up.*

Listen to this one.
CATE: ?
BELINDA: [*sultry and suggestively*] Hi there.
Oh, hi Eddie,
is that what your friends call you?
Eddie the man, Eddie the king.
Is that what they call you, Eddie?
What's my name?
What do you want my name to be, Eddie baby?
Sure, my real name—sure, baby, my name's Nakita?

>   CATE *laughs.*

My name's Nakita, Na-Kita, get your mouth around that one, baby.
Can you get your mouth around it, baby, show me how?
Go on, let me hear you say it.
NA—KI—TA.

>   *The girls are both silently laughing, trying not to be heard.*

SCENE 7

Can be spoken by any actor or surtitled:

>   'Once nerve cells are damaged they start to misfire and the body experiences false touch sensations that are merely the result of damaged receptors.'

SASKIA *and* CAMERON.

At their place.

SASKIA *is on a continuing rampage.*
She stops and looks directly at him.

SASKIA: You fuck!

    He looks away.

Look at me!
She's my boss!
You got angry with me!
'She might have some stupid crush.'
I was mortified. My boss.
You encouraged me
to feel sorry for her.
I fucking even felt a little bit smug.
Smug!
You lied to / me.

CAMERON: I'm telling you the truth now.

    He starts moving away.

SASKIA: Don't you dare walk away,
we stay here, right here,
until,
until we decide what to do,
that's the deal, Cameron.
Yes, that's right, all night
if that's what it takes—

CAMERON: I don't know / what to say.

SASKIA: / Tell me it didn't happen.
Please just tell me you didn't do this.

CAMERON: You are completely right
to be furious with me. /

SASKIA: Don't tell me what my rights are—
Oh, my God!
She told me last week
I wasn't up to a promotion.
Me!

I sat there like some fucking little girl and thought maybe she's right,
maybe I'm not good enough,
maybe—
I didn't know all the while
she was sitting there hating me
because you hadn't left me.
Yet.

CAMERON: I would never leave you.

> CAMERON *tries to touch her.*
>
> *She won't let him.*
>
> *Pause.*
>
> SASKIA *starts the interrogation:*

SASKIA: How many times?

> *Silence*

How many times? /
CAMERON: *Once!*
SASKIA: Once?
CAMERON: Once. A terrible mistake.
SASKIA: How many times?
CAMERON: [*defensive*] God, Saskia! Once.

> *Silence.*

SASKIA: Are you lying to me?
CAMERON: You have to believe me.
SASKIA: Believe you?
CAMERON: It was a stupid one night stand,
   meant nothing. Was nothing.
SASKIA: Nothing?
   You had sex with someone else.
CAMERON: You're blowing it out of proportion.
SASKIA: You're doing it again.
   Suddenly it's me that— /
CAMERON: I'll never lie to you again.

> *Beat.*

SASKIA: Okay.

Pause.

When?

Pause.

CAMERON: Ages ago.
SASKIA: I need to know when?

Perhaps during SASKIA's *interrogation of* CAMERON *she holds his hand in a fist and when he doesn't answer her question she hits herself with his fist forcing him to either physically hurt her or emotionally hurt her.*

CAMERON: —
SASKIA: When? How? Why?
CAMERON: Don't, Saskia.
Don't do this to yourself.
To us.
SASKIA: When?

Pause.

CAMERON: The night of my book launch.
SASKIA: Your launch—?
But I was there—?
All our friends—
Oh God.
I left early so one of us would show up at *your* fucking autistic nephew's end-of-year concert.
So *he* would feel supported!

Silence.

Then the next part of the interrogation:

Where?
CAMERON: No.
SASKIA: Did you fuck her in my bed?
In our bed? /
CAMERON: Of course not.
SASKIA: 'No, of course not.'
I don't believe you! /
CAMERON: Her apartment.

SASKIA: Oh God, you went with her
   to her apartment.
CAMERON: You asked me, I'm telling you the truth.

   SASKIA *continues.*

SASKIA: Why?

   A moment.

CAMERON: Why? I don't—
   She was going to lend me a book.
SASKIA: What book?
CAMERON: I don't know.
SASKIA: So what happened
   when you got up there?
CAMERON: [*with a groan*] What the fuck!
SASKIA: You said you would be
   honest with me.

   Silence.

Tell me or I walk out this door.

   She threatens to go.

CAMERON: Okay. She just poured me some drink.
SASKIA: What was it?
CAMERON: Saskia, I don't remember.
SASKIA: *What?!*
CAMERON: I don't know.
SASKIA: Yes you do! /
CAMERON: Tequila shot.

   Pause.

SASKIA: Okay, so then what?
   After the tequila?
CAMERON: —
SASKIA: I
   need
   you
   to tell me.
CAMERON: —
SASKIA: *Tell me!*

CAMERON: We sat on that, that ugly daybed thing she has. I was drunk.
SASKIA: On the bed.
CAMERON: *Day* bed.
SASKIA: With her?

    Silence.

And?
CAMERON: I was drunk, she was all over me.
SASKIA: Yes of course—she was
  all over you!

    Pause.

CAMERON: She was!
SASKIA: [*parodying him/men*] 'It's not my fault',
  'I was drunk and she was all over me',
  'It's not my fault'.

    Beat.

So.
Tell me how it started.
CAMERON: What?
SASKIA: The sex, Cameron.
  Tell me how it started /
CAMERON: I don't know.
  It started how these things start.

    A moment.

She kissed me.

    Beat.

SASKIA: She kissed you.

    Silence.

And you kissed her back.
CAMERON: —
SASKIA: Then what?
CAMERON: Oh God, it just fucking happened.
SASKIA: Did you, did you take her clothes off?
CAMERON: No. /
SASKIA: So how did you manage to get your fucking cock inside her?

CAMERON: Oh God.
SASKIA: You stripped her clothes off her!
CAMERON: *No*, she just, I don't know,
 she just took her underwear off.
SASKIA: [*defeated*] She took her underwear off.
CAMERON: I can't do this.
SASKIA: So you went to her apartment,
 she took her underwear off
 and you fucked her.

> *He barely nods.*
>
> *A moment.*
>
> *The interrogation resumes:*

How?

> CAMERON *groans in disbelief.*

How?
CAMERON: Don't— /
SASKIA: Did you go down on her?
CAMERON: *No.*
SASKIA: Did she go down on you?
 Did she take your cock in her mouth?
 Did you put your hands
 up her cunt?
 Did you, did you?

> *He won't answer.*

Okay I'm going.
CAMERON: I can't remember /
SASKIA: *Can't remember?!*
CAMERON: I didn't, no. *No!* /
SASKIA: Did you make that sound you make,
 the one in your throat? /
CAMERON: God. /
SASKIA: The one only I hear? /
CAMERON: No. /
SASKIA: What did she smell like? What did Rochelle smell like? Did she smell like sweet jasmine, did she? Did she smell all musky and warm?

Oh yes, all hot and sweet musky sweat. Or did she smell like fish, like squid, her cunt like rotting fish? /

CAMERON: [*groaning*] Oh God, please, Saskia, don't. /

SASKIA: Did you kiss her breasts? /

CAMERON: I don't know! *No!* /

SASKIA: Did you suck her nipples into your mouth, your tongue lingering over them, latch onto them like a fucking baby? *Did you?!* Did you stick your hard fucking 'big' cock between her breasts, did she gasp and moan and look at you with that 'come to me, baby' look? Did she? Did you? Did you fuck her from behind, or on top? Up against the wall, over the bed. Did you? Did you do all that? /

CAMERON: No, no, *no, no!*

Of course not.

I would never do all that stuff—

No!

>   *Beat.*

SASKIA: You just lay with her and
you stuck your cock in her,
is that it?

>   CAMERON *blank.*

Answer me.

>   *He nods.*

>   *She physically and emotionally slumps.*

God. Really? You really did.
You did that?

>   *Silence.*

I feel sick.

SCENE 8

AREZU: It's 3:00 a.m. and I'm vomiting in the street outside my house
mascara down my face
left one of my shoes in the cab

I haven't told my parents I've dropped out of university

I'm in a dark dark place
deep inside me something is wrong
I can't feel anything
nothing touches me.

Start working a shitty job
partying and drinking each night

my parents and me
we fight all the time
and in one enormous argument they yell

'We came to this country so you could be free.
This is not the life we dreamt for you.'

So much screaming

all we do is hurt each other
each line accusation like a slap.

I go to my room
slam the door hard
pack my things in a frenzy

kicking walls
hurling my childhood books across the room
and then—

I find the poetry book Mosa gave me

stop

and

read words that feel gentle

like the touch of a hand holding my heart

beautiful words
in English and in Farsi

> *These words by Hafez in English or in Farsi will be projected about the space:*
> *'This love you have for the Truth will never forsake you,*
> *Your joys and sufferings are like rising stage curtain and will surely reveal your magnificent self.'*

and I am transported

I feel myself

> *She wraps herself in pages of poetry.*

wrapped in poetry.

SCENE 9

Can be spoken by any actor or surtitled:

> '*At death the human organism ceases to register touch, but for a short time after death, electrical impulses continue to travel around the body, carrying information to an unresponsive brain.*'

MARK *is working—he seems to be back in surgery (at least that is what the audience should think at first).*

He is dressed in surgical gear, hovering over a 'patient' on the table.

He has a surgical mask on.

There is heavy music playing as MARK *works on the patient.*

He is different.

Rough, less focused, disrespectful, angry.

Alone, working on this still person.

At various stages he takes pieces of leftover flesh and throws them like a small basketball into the biological waste bin.

When he gets it in he roars a goal.

LIBBY *enters. She holds a surgical mask over her nose and mouth and tentatively approaches* MARK.

He doesn't look but hears her approach.

MARK: You shouldn't be in here.
LIBBY: It's nearly midnight!

> MARK *holds something up—flesh of some type.*
>
> *Takes his mask off, leaving the mask dangling around his neck and laughs.*

MARK: Guess?

> LIBBY *retches.*

She turns off the music.

You'll get used to the smell.

Silence as he challenges her with his face.

LIBBY: This is horrible.
You don't belong here.

MARK: —

> MARK *nonchalantly throws another organ through the basketball hoop. Cheers or jeers depending on whether he gets it in.*

LIBBY: Mark, you lost a patient,
It happens to surgeons all the time,
It's part of the job. /

MARK: No!

LIBBY: You're not fucking God. /

MARK: Libby, I'm working.

LIBBY: —

MARK: I'll be home later.

LIBBY: —

MARK: I need you to go.

LIBBY: —

MARK: Get out.

LIBBY: It's pathetic.

MARK: I said get out.

Get out!

> MARK *goes to push her. So close, he stops himself.*

LIBBY: Go on then.

She pushes herself up against him. Hard and rough.

Come on, grab my arm—
Touch my skin, go on, feel it,
feel the heat of me.

Her skin, her flesh, her smell, her sex.

He recoils and retreats.

Go on—
Put your hands on me,
hit me, scratch me, feel the pulse of me.

She goes to grab his hand and put it on her heart, but he pulls away, roughly, afraid.

She suddenly realises what the issue is.

Oh, my God—
You can't—

> MARK *looks at her threateningly while holding an organ that he is squishing through his hands. She backs against a wall.*

He pushes the organ into her—her body, her face.

MARK: Feel it.
　Still.
　Cold.
　Empty.
　That's all there is.
LIBBY: Stop it, stop it.
　What's wrong with you?
　Feel *me!*
　I'm alive!

He backs right off.

She sees this.

She leaves the room.

He throws the organ limply through the hoop.

Does he laugh?

Does he then direct his self-hatred at the body before him?

Fury, pain, cold.

SCENE 10

ALICE *is at the sink—a Sunlight lemon dish soap packet on the shelf next to her. She starts to wash the dishes.*

Is there is a kitchen timer running?

ALICE: The sun shines hot yellow in a pure sky.
　I catch him and he giggles as I throw him up again.
　Trusting me.

Up up he goes and I catch him in my arms.
Again.
His blonde hair floating in the breeze.
His laughter making me braver.
Then—
Then I don't catch him.
He falls into the water,
it's shallow, but I—

> *She drops the soap/washcloth in the water and cannot find it. She frantically searches through the water.*
>
> *Does she hit a kitchen timer and it starts to count down for two minutes?*

The waves are getting rougher and the water it's getting deeper, the sky closes in, and—
And I'm looking and looking
and counting—67, 68, 69,
because I know there's only 120 seconds,
two minutes before—
95, 96, 97.

I think I can hear him crying under the water,
but I can't see him…
117, 118, 119…

> *Ambulance siren at the same time as…*
>
> *The kitchen alarm goes off loudly—two minutes is up.*
>
> *She turns it off.*

They took him right back to the hospital where he was born
like he was only on loan.
An oxygen mask over his tiny face,
I won't leave the hospital,
not to sleep, eat, shower—
Never leave his bedside.

Wake up
covered in sweat,
and he's lying there with the tube through his tiny nose,

the weeny cast on his little left arm that holds the drip into him.
And he's whimpering.

> *Does an image of* PETER *walk in during all this crisis and stand there? This is the first time that we see him. When she sees him…*

I wrap myself around him!

> *She wraps her arms around him.*

I'm crying all over him—
So relieved that he's there.
He's going to be okay,
so grateful.
That I have another chance with him.

> PETER *leaves.*

SCENE 11

Silence.

More silence.

Silence.

CAMERON: It was a terrible filthy mistake.
Look at me.

> *She can't look.*

You are the one I adore,
the one I love.
SASKIA: But you fucked *her!*
CAMERON: Yes okay. Yes. *Yes!*
How many times
do you want me to say it?
I fucked her.
Does it make you feel better?
SASKIA: Don't—
CAMERON: Before we were married, you—
SASKIA: *Before!*

> *Beat.*

Cameron, am I not enough for you?

CAMERON: Baby, don't say that.
SASKIA: What then? Did you not find me
attractive anymore?
CAMERON: No. No. Nothing like that.
You are the most
beautiful woman ever.
SASKIA: I hate my stupid innocent self.
CAMERON: Don't hate you, hate me.
Me. /
SASKIA: Oh I do.
I hate you.
I hate you so much.

She is vulnerable.

CAMERON seizes the moment.

He tries to console her somewhat.

CAMERON: I knew I had fucked up everything—
And I know
this doesn't excuse me,
but I stopped halfway.
SASKIA: You what?
CAMERON: I saw myself in this awful thing,
and I—
I stopped,
I couldn't go through with it.
SASKIA: You didn't—?
CAMERON: I didn't come.

SASKIA laughs slightly hysterically, which then tails into a sob.

Saskia. I feel wretched.
If I could take it away I would,
if you want me to go—
You want me to go, don't you, Sas?
SASKIA: That's what's killing me.
I don't want you to go,
I hate you. I love you.
I want to fuck this out of you,
scrub your body clean.

CAMERON *goes to stroke her.*

She pulls away from him violently.

Don't touch me.
CAMERON: —
SASKIA: —
CAMERON: —

She loses her violence.

Asks one final sad question:

SASKIA: Did you have your jeans off or on?
CAMERON: What?
SASKIA: Don't stall.
CAMERON: What difference does it? /
SASKIA: Off or on?
CAMERON: The whole thing was so sordid, so—
SASKIA: Just—
Off or on?

Silence.

CAMERON: I don't know.
SASKIA: —
CAMERON: —
SASKIA: —?
CAMERON: Off.
SASKIA: Oh.

Silence.

SCENE 12

Can be spoken by any actor or surtitled:

'Touch receptors send electricity along nerve cells toward the central nervous system.

If a touch causes extreme pain, synapses fire at higher rates, neural messages of alarm are sent to many parts of the body.'

AREZU *is bathing or being bathed by a group of women.*

A metaphoric start of something new.

AREZU: I go on a journey
> reading poems
>
> and everything about the country my parents left
> everything about Iran comes alive for me.
>
> I learn Farsi
> go to political meetings
> wearing the hijab when I need to
>
> I am consumed with yearning
>
> My parents won't talk to me about it
> instead my mother shouts at me
> 'Your name means "Hope"
> we brought you here for a future
> not politics and worries
>
> you're *our* hope'.
>
> But I tell her my name belongs to me now
>
> that they took me here to be free
> but I am not free
> I tell them
> I'm going to Iran
> to join the struggle
> that I need to know my homeland
> to know who I am
> just because they fled
> doesn't mean I don't belong there.
> I will go and
> I will fight for freedom
> fight for the freedom they gave up on
>
> before I feel it
> my mother cries
>
> there is this weight I suddenly cannot bear
>
> then when she tries to hug me
> I can't take it anymore
> I feel this force inside me
> pushing her away

my hands gripping her shoulders
hard with force

and in that moment
in that meeting of skin and muscle against skin and muscle
something between us is broken.

SCENE 13

MARK *is on the phone to* CATE.

Is he alone in the spotlight?

Holds the phone.

Does he caress the phone at times?

Is the next scene of SASKIA *bathing* CAMERON *also starting on stage during this scene?*

There is nothing sexual about MARK*'s call.*

MARK: Hello.
 Um, I'm Doctor—
 Mark, just call me Mark.
 I've never called anywhere like this before.
 No, no please don't, I don't want—
 Look, I just wanted to talk to you.
 Just ask you some—
 I mean if you don't mind.
 Can you do something for me? Please.

 The person on the other end tries sexual talk.

No no, no, nothing like that.
Did you know that when someone touches you, say... your forearm— /

 Not heard, but the other person says, 'forearm?' /

Yes your forearm. If you run your fingertips down your forearm.
Yes, yes that's right, can you do that for me?
Did you know that while you are doing that, that there are hundreds of synapses firing in your brain, registering all the messages coming directly from receptor cells beneath your skin?

Can you do it again, just with the softest fingertips? Run them over your forearm and under your wrist.
No not to me, to yourself.
Can you feel the veins and arteries, can you feel them pulsing?
Can you touch your own arm just with your fingertips and tell me—
Tell me what it feels like?

—

Makes you shiver, yes? And?
Does it feel warm?

—

Can you, can you just hold onto your forearm for me please?
Yes like that, hold the flesh of it.
Wrap your hand and fingers around the skin, the muscle, the tissue, like you're not going to let go.
Don't cause any pain though.
Is it causing pain?
Good.
Can you tell me what it feels like?
Yes, that's right, all those receptor cells, but I don't mean that.
I mean, can you tell me how you actually feel?
You know, what feeling you get when you are held like that?

—

And do you—? Sorry what was your name?

—

Chantal.
When you have that feeling, the one you said feels alive, feels warm, is it—
Is it beautiful?

> *Blackout on* MARK.
>
> *Lights focus on* SASKIA *bathing* CAMERON.

SCENE 14

Can be spoken by any actor or surtitled:

> *'Touching another is the most intimate of all behaviours.*
>
> *The experience of touching another person creates a language unique to that particular pairing.'*

SASKIA *leads* CAMERON, *removes his clothes until he is naked/near naked, places him into a bath and bathes him.*

The physical act of washing him could begin at the same time as the previous scene and build up to when she speaks in this scene.

The washing of CAMERON *is a long, involved and intimate process.*

A healing is taking place, a reunion, a merging into selves.

SASKIA *is reclaiming him and he is accepting forgiveness.*

It is a ritual, a return.

The washing goes on for an extended time.

It is sensual, almost sexual, completely silent.

As it goes on, a dance, a healing, something magical could happen.

They tentatively kiss, then more hungrily.

She pulls away briefly.

She cries.

He holds her head.

Silence and tears.

More silence and touching.

An exploration of each other, locked in a truly shared moment.

SASKIA: I love you.

> CAMERON *stares at her for a long time.*
>
> *He stops staring and looks away.*
>
> *He lets go of her.*

What?

> *She reaches out to touch him, but he brushes her away.*
>
> *She is confused, alarmed, vulnerable.*

CAMERON: It was more than once.

> *Beat.*

SASKIA: What?
CAMERON: —
SASKIA: I don't—
CAMERON: With her.

Beat.

SASKIA: How many—
CAMERON: I slept with her seven times.
SASKIA: —
CAMERON: I disgust myself
and you should know who I really am.
SASKIA: God!
CAMERON: I went to her place—
One time when you were working
all night on—
On my book, editing my book.
Another time you were away with
your mum.
I fucked her each time.
Swore I would never—
And then went back again
and again.
Weak and pathetic, stupid and—
SASKIA: —
CAMERON: Yes. I did.
Me.
I fucked her and fucked her
sometimes even a few times
in the same night.
I even stayed over at her place twice
when you were away.
I did this to you.
And I have lied and lied—
To your face, while you loved me,
I have lied
right up
until
this moment.
SASKIA: —
CAMERON: I love you and
you should know the man I am.
This is the man I am.

Silence.

SASKIA: You let me—
  Just now.
  With my bare hands.
CAMERON: Yes, I did
  I let you wash me
  and
  I almost
  just now
  let you make love to me.

  Silence.

  SASKIA *stares at him.*

SASKIA: You slept with her seven times?
CAMERON: Jesus, Saskia.
  Yes. *Seven* times.
  That's me.
  That's what I am.

  Beat.

SASKIA: I can't believe you.

  She pulls right back.

  It is the point of no return.

SCENE 15

CATE *is at work on the running machine with headset—she is there on her own for now.*

She is finishing off with a client.

CATE: Slow down, Darcy,
  I need this moment to last,
  I need you to hold that beautiful cock for a bit longer, that's right, that's the way, baby,
  this is the best ever, you are the best ever.
  Yes. Yes. I can feel that.
  Yes, Darcy, you are all man, you are all…
  Okay that was great, sure,

I enjoyed it so much.
Make sure you ask for me, next time.
Ask for Chantal, won't you, Darcy?
Call me real soon, big man, I'll be thinking about you.

She gets a call from a familiar client.

Hi, it's Chantal here—
Oh, Mark…
How are you today?

When she realises who it is she adjusts to a walking pace.

Do you want us to do the same thing we usually do?
No, no, I actually like talking to—
So I'm all ears, I'm listening.
For as long as you like,
yeah.
But you know I shouldn't remind you but
you are paying by the minute, so—
No. No, of course not.
The longer the better for me
I just didn't want you—
In fact I'm usually too fast.
Oh nothing, don't worry.

She puts her hand to her face while on the running machine.

Yes I'm doing it.
Fingertips on my cheek.
Um, small tiny hairs.
Yes they tickle a bit.
It feels soft and sort of velvety,
kind of like a peach, the skin of a peach.
Yes like that.
Tingly,
sort of gentle I guess.

Okay, my whole hand flat on my cheek.
It's a bit tricky while I'm walking but—

No, walking at work, they give us
these running machines.

Um—kind of to keep fit, sort of…
Okay I've got it, hand firmly on my cheek.

> *She has her hand firmly placed on her cheek, flat palm down.*

I can feel my fingers where they rise and fall.
It feels smooth and
warm.
No not cold
not cold at all.
Actually quite hot, I've been
on the machine a while.

> *Her mobile phone rings. It is in her pocket.*

Oh God, Mark, I'm—
I wouldn't normally answer it, it's just that the only people that have this number—
Can I just—
I'll just pop you on hold.

> *She takes the mobile phone out of her pocket. She answers it.*
>
> *She stops walking.*

Oh hi.
Quick, I'm working!
At a… gym.
When are you going to come and see us?

> BELINDA *enters, looks at her questioningly.*
>
> CATE *tries to keep the conversation somewhat private.*

No. God, I don't want money,
I just wanted you to—
You're his uncle and—
He *can't* talk on the phone!
Why do you think?
Because.

> *She loses her sense of where she is and forgets to be private.*

Because—
You know why.

No. That's not—
He's fucking profoundly autistic,
for Christ's sake.
I don't want your fucking money,
I just wanted you to want to come
over sometime.
You know what Cameron—
Forget it.

> *She hangs up.*
>
> *Sees* BELINDA. BELINDA *has heard, she turns and indicates she is going to go fill up her water bottle.*
>
> CATE *goes back to the other phone and starts walking again.*

Hello?
Oh, God. Shit.
I thought you were on hold—

No, nothing—
Shouldn't we get back on the—

Yes, he's seven.

> *Beat.*

No.
Not at all.
Well, a bit—
I mean he's…

> *She stops again on the running machine.*

Mark, can I ask you something?
Why?
Why call here—and talk to me about skin,
and veins and pulses?
It's just—

> *Beat.*

This is a sex line!

SCENE 16

AREZU: I catch a train to Melbourne [*UK version:* Manchester] to meet with Mosa
he has his own child now, a tiny baby girl
when I talk to him he fades away
he is building his Australian [*UK version:* English] life and doesn't want to think about old conversations
he tells me that he doesn't read poetry anymore
Mosa says he can't go back
it's too late for him
and he's not sure he now trusts what he used to believe.

But he writes down the contact details
of people i can go to
in Teheran
then there is nothing for us to talk about.

I jump back on the train and then it hits me
like electricity
I realise
it was me all along
who would return.

When I tell my father I am going
he looks ashen
reasons with me
bargains with me
starts to beg
but I cannot be budged
I want to go there, ask questions
find out everything
know who I am
he says that if I go
I will be in danger

but I am sick of all this fear
his fear
my mother's fear

I want to be free of this.

Pause.

My father stands before me
he tells me of a young married couple
educated and optimistic
filled with political passion
idealism
fighting for a secular State
where religion was private
And State matters were separate

he tells me of meeting in secret locations

there is a silence

and then
he tells me
what happened to her
my mother

he tells it without flourish
her—
Incarceration
and—
What happened to her in prison
the degradation, the—

He has been forced to tell me what she wants to forget

and I remember Mosa's sad eyes
how he seemed to know about
my mother
and my past

and how I came to be.

My father stands there waiting
but there are no words

for the first time
there are no words.

SCENE 17

SASKIA *is packing her belongings.*

CAMERON *is in the room watching.*

SASKIA *comes across items that* CAMERON *has given her—what do you do with those?*

Possibly Scenes 17 and 18 can run in tandem, choreographed with overlapping lines as two characters pack. Alternatively, the suitcase half packed by SASKIA *can be taken over by* MARK *packing in Scene 18.*

SASKIA: And when I fuck someone else
then—then maybe you will know,
know this feeling,
at least a little bit of it,
make you hurt.
Think about
how I touched him,
what he tasted like,
what his body made mine do,
how I kissed him,
licked him,
caressed him.
And only then, after all that
when you understand
can feel this—this,
this... ache
only then
could we be equal again.

Because our equal is burnt and ruined

and so there is nowhere for us now.

You don't get to touch me again
put your hands near me—
Kiss me—
Reach for my breasts,
feel the wet between my legs.

And yet

> *She struggles.*

it's all still fucking there.
This desire.
This memory of your warm back against my belly, the soft flutter of your chest hairs through my fingers, my toes coiled around yours.

I still know your skin texture, the smell of you infused with love and yet now
a fresh living repulsion.
The touch of you
alive and palpable,

a somatic memory
of
absolutely
no
use.

CAMERON: Where are you going?
SASKIA: —
CAMERON: Where will you go?
SASKIA: —
CAMERON: Please, Saskia /
SASKIA: It's no longer any of your business.

> *Beat.*

Don't call me.

> SASKIA *picks up the bag and leaves. (Or it is left for* MARK *to continue packing in Scene 18.)*
>
> CAMERON *reaches out to her.*
>
> *She leaves him alone.*

SCENE 18

LIBBY *and* MARK.

Perhaps they are standing in the same mess that SASKIA *was standing in previously.*

MARK *has a dictaphone in his hand. He records himself speaking.*

MARK: All human organisms experience touch differently. The number of receptors at a somatic site determine the different experiences of exactly the same stimuli.

> *This is the first time the audience has made the connection between* MARK *and the very personal journey he is taking in dissecting the medical and intellectual ideas on human touch.*
>
> *The recordings/titles throughout the play would now make sense in terms of them being part of this journey.*
>
> *He finishes recording, turns the dictaphone off and throws it into the suitcase/bag. Then he starts to pack his clothes.*
>
> MARK *continues packing—is he leaving* LIBBY*?*
>
> *Is* LIBBY *stripping the bed as he packs?*
>
> *There is a cold distance between them. Any accidental contact is avoided by* MARK*.*
>
> *Silence.*

LIBBY: So you are definitely going—

> *Beat.*

Singapore?

MARK: Unfortunately yes.

LIBBY: Singapore.

MARK: —

LIBBY: So just go in and tell them you're not going.
That you don't want to go.

MARK: —

LIBBY: I mean, Mark, come on
this isn't what you gave up surgery for.
They must know that.

> MARK *keeps packing.*

Tell them you need to get back into your surgical practice that you're finishing your time at the Coroner's office.

> MARK *continues packing, ignoring her.*

I mean this is not what you really want for your life, is it?

MARK: —

LIBBY: Talk to me.
MARK: —
LIBBY: My God, you *want* to go!

> MARK *pauses. He looks at her. There is no denial of this.*

Talk to me!

> MARK *finishes packing, closes the bag.*

Okay, so you go, Mark,
because, you know what?
You can't stay here.
Not like this.

SCENE 19

AREZU *is on a bus.*

AREZU: The 400 bus takes the long way to the airport
from Rockdale through Banksia and Arncliffe
along streets that I know like my own skin

I press my face against the window as it weaves past my Australian childhood

hurtling through the only city that I have ever known.

My phone is on silent but I feel the vibrations of missed calls and texts.

Words sent in silence

I won't listen to the messages or read the texts
I cannot bear to hear my mother's voice

I'm leaving today
on a plane to Teheran
a flight to belonging

I want to bring hope
with me.

[*UK version:*
I board the Heathrow express at Paddington
fifteen minutes to the airport

grab a coffee from Nero
and settle my case down in the luggage rack

I listen as a voice in my own accent tells me when we will arrive at the terminal.
Hurtle through the only city that I have ever known.
Watch as my childhood stretches behind me.

My phone is on silent but I feel the vibrations of missed calls and texts.

Words sent to me in silence

I won't listen to the messages or read the texts
I cannot bear to hear my mother's voice

I'm leaving today
on a plane to Teheran
a flight to belonging

I want to bring hope
with me.]

SCENE 20

ALICE *is on an empty aircraft. She clutches a photo.*

A British Airways FLIGHT ATTENDANT *approaches her.*

FLIGHT ATTENDANT: Excuse me, ma'am, you have to disembark now.
 We have arrived at our destination.
 We're here!
 We've landed in Singapore.
 You're the last passenger on board, ma'am.
 Holidays to be had!
ALICE: My son.
FLIGHT ATTENDANT: Your son? You're here to visit him.
 Lovely.
ALICE: Yes he is lovely
 he's all I've got.

   She shows her a photo.

 When he was little.

FLIGHT ATTENDANT: Lovely. What a lovely baby.
Do you need help with your bags?

She does.

ALICE: Eight pounds two ounces
twenty inches long,
he came out all blue and then he just sort of lit up.
Pink.
Loved him the moment—
I cried, wept.
From nowhere this little person,
heart thumping at the brutality of birth,
lips on my breasts
and then a wonderful little boy.
A world of bandaids, haircuts,
storybooks, soccer games,
girlfriends, broken hearts, drunken vomiting,
head laid across my arm,
movies and TV dinners,
birthday candles,
tears and smiles and—
And now.
This. /

FLIGHT ATTENDANT: He's lovely, just lovely.
And I'm afraid I really must insist that you disembark the aircraft now.
That's right. Thanks so much.
And you have a lovely time here, won't you?
With your son.
Thank you for travelling with us today.

ALICE *disembarks.*

ALICE: Ten stone two pounds
five foot eleven inches.
In less than fifty hours and nineteen minutes this foreign nation will take my son,
will place a rope around his throat,
hang him until his neck breaks
and his heart stops beating.

Will kill my boy
for his crime of carrying a stupid decision into
their land.
Their land.
They are going to force me,
his mother,
to outlive my darling boy.
And even now,
as a last act of torture
they won't let me touch him,
they won't let me touch him!
Hold him,
kiss him.
They won't let me stroke his cheek
feel his heart beating
please…
let me lay his head against my breast one last time.
They think they own his life, and his death,
but they don't
they don't.
He belongs to me.
I'm his mother
his mum
his flesh belongs to me.

   Pause.

I have been forced to accept so much
but not this,
not this last denial.
I can't.

I need to breathe him in,
breathe it in,
this last moment

SCENE 21

At Cate's house.

ADAM, *Cate's son, is having a bad tantrum.*

CATE *is struggling.*

BELINDA *is clutching a bottle of wine!*

CATE: We could ring for pizza.
BELINDA: Love it.

>ADAM *hurtles something at* CATE*'s head.*

Jesus, Cate.
CATE: He doesn't mean it,
just a bad day.
BELINDA: Yes of course,
good days and bad days,
that's how it goes with all kids, isn't it?
CATE: Adam, this is Mummy's friend.
Belinda.

>ADAM *doesn't take any interest and continues thrashing around.*

Belinda works with Mummy.

>ADAM *throws things at* CATE.

BELINDA: Ooh dear, be careful, mate.
CATE: It's fine, he doesn't mean it.

>*He throws things again.* CATE *gets hit by some. This time it really hurts.*

So much goes on,
he can only tell me this way.
BELINDA: So, what, he just throws stuff?
CATE: No, well yes,
but he doesn't mean to hurt me.
It's a form of communication in a way.
BELINDA: [*unconvinced*] Oh, of course.
CATE: Pepperoni or Hawaiian?

>ADAM *throws something at* CATE *again.*

BELINDA: Hey, come on now, buddy,
enough of that.

>ADAM *looks at* BELINDA.

CATE: He feels nervous with strangers.
He's a bit scared of you.

BELINDA: [*trying to make a joke*] Well, to be honest seeing things flying around the room makes me a bit scared of him.

 ADAM *throws his dinner across the room.*

 BELINDA *looks on in horror as* CATE *tries unsuccessfully to clean up the mess while* ADAM *goes further into rampage mode.*

Jesus, Cate—
Do you ever— /
CATE: No.
BELINDA: What?
CATE: —
BELINDA: You can't live like this.
He's not—
This is worse than— /
CATE: It's about loving him, Belinda.
BELINDA: Yes yes, of course but—
CATE: Imagine being him, trapped in his world where everything is out of your control, where you don't understand what's happening.

 BELINDA *gives her a look.*

Don't.
[*To* ADAM] It's okay, darling, Adam, Mummy isn't going anywhere.
[*To* BELINDA] There's more to him than you're seeing.
BELINDA: Don't take this the wrong way,
but I really hope so!

 Silence as they watch ADAM.

CATE: It's just a tantrum.
He's anxious.
BELINDA: I'm going to tell you straight,
this is crazy,
it's not liveable
CATE: He's a monster?
BELINDA: No I—
CATE: A monster, a waste of my life.
A semi-person. A liability.
I know it's what everyone thinks.
BELINDA: You're angry with me.

Beat.

CATE: Yes.
No.
Yes.

Beat.

Yes. Fucking don't.
Of course I'm angry,

I'm angry that—
That I haven't made him better.
And it might not get—
Ever.

BELINDA: —

CATE: I'm angry at the world,
with my friends for calling less,
with myself for being here,
with my brother for giving up on him.
Sometimes I'm so angry
it turns to hate.
And I yell back at Adam,
scream back.
And the worst is,
the worst thing is he barely notices.

Beat.

But then—
When he's calm
and I run my fingers down his back,
when I do that, he makes this noise.

She makes a pleased noise.

She smiles.

And the way he looks at me,
touches my face,
like an angel,
like a wizard.
Wise.
Seeing something, feeling something

that no-one else sees, feels.
We can sit like that for hours,
sitting in his world.
Together.
>*Beat.*

You think I'm crazy, don't you?
>*Pause.*

BELINDA: To be honest, yes.
You see what you want,
but the truth is,
Cate, he's not—
It's awful, you're young,
you can't survive this.
CATE: I know, I know
it's not much,
compared to other mothers
and what they get.
But, Belinda,
when he does that—
BELINDA: What?
CATE: It's stupid, it's just when
I can reach him like that,
get into that body,
it's stupid but—
Well, I, I go into orbit.
BELINDA: —

>ADAM *suddenly flares up again, and throws something at* CATE. *Her wine glass is hit and her wine is all over her.*

CATE: Shit.
Keep an eye on him,
I'll get a new shirt /
BELINDA: Hurry.

>CATE *has left.* ADAM *starts acting out badly. He picks up some more of his dinner and throws it over his head, he is visibly distressed.* BELINDA *has no idea what to do.*

Okay, mate, enough of that for one night.

>ADAM *gets worse, he is very distressed.*

Oh, God.
Jesus, just stop.
Stop!
Adam, take it easy.
[*Calling out*] Cate, Cate, you there?
It's okay, Adam, I'm Belinda,
Mummy's friend from work.
You know, where Mummy goes running every day.

>*He starts to rock hard against the wall.*

Don't do that, Adam.
Please.

>*He rocks harder, gesticulating wildly.*
>
>*He picks up items and throws them at* BELINDA.

Fuck!
No that is totally not on.
Okay. You hear me.

>ADAM *is still upset, but* BELINDA *approaches him and he slows down and watches her.*

Actually, fuck it,
I know how you feel.
Life sucks.
Especially for you,
but for me too.
So I know how you feel.
Except that you have sauce
all over your face,
so it's kind of hard to take
you seriously.

>ADAM *still rocks but more quietly and listens to her.*
>
>BELINDA *sits down beside him.*
>
>ADAM *turns away.*

Let me get that shit off your face.

BELINDA *takes out a tissue to wipe his face.*

At some point CATE *returns but hangs back, unobserved, watching the interaction between* BELINDA *and* ADAM.

ADAM *reaches out to grab the tissue, and in doing so actually feels* BELINDA*'s face.*

BELINDA *starts and goes to move.*

Then...

That's my face, Adam.

He is intrigued, intense, focused on her face and nothing else.

I don't think you should—

She goes to take his hands off of her face.

When his expression changes, she changes her mind and puts his hands back on her face. She is intrigued, feels herself being touched with curiosity, with awe.

With his hand on her nose, ADAM *looks her in the eyes.*

Nose. That's my nose.

ADAM*'s hands move to her eye.*

Eye, that's my eye.
How I see you.
See, open, closed, open closed.

ADAM *thinks about this for a moment then laughs.*

BELINDA *doesn't get it, but eventually she also laughs.*

SCENE 22

MARK *is in Singapore.*
He is in an official room with ALICE.
Hot.
Tropical.
Overhead fans—noise and air—cutting through the light.
Nothingness.

Sweat.

Anxiety.

Alienation.

MARK: I know it's—
It's extremely difficult.
But I'm afraid there is
nothing I can do about it.
Our government
have made many requests,
they've agitated very strongly.
But I'm afraid we must abide by the laws
of *this* land.
ALICE: But why? Why would they want this as well?
I just can't for the life of me understand it
tell them I just need a minute
tell them—
A few seconds
MARK: It's the policy here in Singapore.
I've read the legislation, there's certain processes that are just not allowed /
ALICE: Please
I'm his mother.

    MARK *nods.*

Did you tell them that?
I'm his mother.
The Australian [*UK version:* British] government,
the Prime Minister,
our people,
they won't let them deny me this,
will they?
You'll fight till they let me.
You'll fight?
Won't you?
MARK: It's so hot here.
ALICE: Are others coming or is—?
MARK: Stifling.

ALICE: Is it just you?
MARK: No, no. There are
many people,
important people—
Politicians, human
rights activists,
parliament itself /
ALICE: It's too late for them
nothing they've done has worked
there is only you left /
MARK: All the right people are watching from home, and all around the world people are so outraged. /
ALICE: Yes but he's my son. My son.
You have to tell them.
MARK: The humidity,
it's hard to breathe, isn't it?
ALICE: Everyone's given up
just like they gave up fighting for his life,
now they've given up fighting for this one small thing.
Haven't they, doctor?
MARK: —
ALICE: I have a right, a mother's right.
MARK: Members of the Australian [*UK version:* British] government are advocating as strongly as they can.
ALICE: But there's no time.
Surely they can't do this,
stop me from touching him?
You must tell them—
MARK: I'm afraid it's not my place to /
ALICE: Please.
MARK: If it was—
ALICE: I'm begging you, please.
MARK: I'm sorry,
I have tried
but it's just not my place.
ALICE: Not your place? You're a doctor.
You're part of the government, aren't you?

MARK: No I'm just—
ALICE: They'll listen to you.
MARK: There's just nothing I can do.
ALICE: You won't do anything. You're giving in.
MARK: I can't do anything.
ALICE: I'm begging you!
MARK: I can't, I can't—
ALICE: Imagine if it was your child, someone you loved?
MARK: *I'm not God!*

>*Pause.*

Sorry.
ALICE: Please.

>*Beat.*

I just want to hug my boy.

SCENE 23

International Airport

Arrival and departure information.

Other actors wheeling bags across the space—human traffic.

Amongst the harried crowd sit AREZU *and* SASKIA

Not near, not far.

The long rows of seats are vacant but for them, yet people are moving everywhere, all around.

They don't talk, or particularly connect, but their energy is there
in the same place
together
with the noise of the announcements and the ordered chaos that is Sydney's Kingsford Smith [UK version: London's Heathrow].

After a long time (and after announcements paging passenger Saskia Dawson) SASKIA *gets up to leave.*

Has she missed her flight or does she rush to make it?

SASKIA *takes hold of her wheelie bag.*

Now she is rushing to leave and trips over AREZU *as she passes.*

She falls, her stuff going everywhere.

AREZU *jumps up to help pick her up.*

To help collect her stuff.

AREZU: I am so sorry.
SASKIA: No, no, it's me, I was distracted.

>*They come into physical contact.*

AREZU: Are you alright?

>*She helps* SASKIA *up, helps pick up her things.*

SASKIA: Yes. I—
　I'm fine,
　I'm, I'm fine.

>AREZU *picks up the papers that have fallen out of Saskia's bag. She looks at them. They are pages of poetry.*
>
>AREZU *smiles and hands them over.*
>
>*There is a moment.*
>
>*Eyes meet.*
>
>*They connect fully.*

AREZU: Moafagh bashed. Good luck.
SASKIA: Thank you. You too.

>*A moment.*
>
>AREZU *goes back to her seat.*
>
>SASKIA *watches her.*
>
>*Everyone else leaves.*
>
>*Quiet.*
>
>SASKIA*'s body takes a moment.*
>
>*She sighs.*
>
>*Sits back down.*

She just needs time to be…

SASKIA *sits there alone with her thoughts.*

AREZU *looks over at* SASKIA *then back to her own thoughts.*

SCENE 24

Dawn.
In a filthy Singaporean prison cell.
Smell.
Heat.
Sweat.
Stress.
Tension.
PETER *and* MARK.

PETER: They won't let her.
 Let her hold me before, will they?
MARK: They're very strict / here.
PETER: / Yes.
MARK: I'm afraid there are rules
 that have to be obeyed /
PETER: Will she be there?

 Beat.

MARK: No, not at the actual—
 Event.
PETER: Afterwards?
MARK: Yes. I assume she will
 be allowed access to the… site,
 after the paperwork.
PETER: Paperwork?
MARK: There are documents that
 have to be finalised.
 I have to sign the—
 Have to complete the Australian [*UK version:* Home]
 Coroner's paperwork.

PETER: And you—
You'll be the only one doing
the 'paperwork'?
MARK: Yes.
PETER: So you'll be with me afterwards.

> MARK *nods.*

Good.

> *Beat.*

You'll be there when they do it?
When they put the rope—
MARK: Yes I'm expected to witness it.
PETER: It will be good to get it over
I guess.
MARK: —
PETER: I've had so many
dreams about it.
Funny things, being on a
road that was hot and dusty
and I had to walk to the end
with chains around my ankles
so they could push me over
a cliff, but they kept getting
lost and there was no
more water… silly stuff.
MARK: —
PETER: And other ones about the
rope getting stuck and I'm
just hanging there while
they tried to make it work.
Sorry.
MARK: —
PETER: —
MARK: Peter
your case has really
angered people—
All over the world.

Politicians are condemning it.
However—
PETER: It's going to happen.
MARK: It is.
PETER: It's not as bad, this part, as in
my dreams.
It's strangely calm really, isn't it?

> *Beat.*

MARK: I'm afraid, as a representative
of the Coroner's Office,
I am required to get some
details from you to make
sure they don't make a mistake.
PETER: Mistake?
MARK: I have to take a measurement
of your, your neck and take
details of your weight, so what
you dreamt of—you know,
getting stuck—so it
doesn't happen.
PETER: Oh, sure.

> *He offers his neck for measuring. After a moment* MARK *does the job. Very carefully with a tape measure somehow managing not to touch him, and writes it down.* MARK *stops and looks at* PETER. *Does he want to somehow apologise? But why?*

It's alright.
I'm ready.

> *Beat.*

MARK: How?
PETER: I don't know how.
Nervous.
But I've thought about it for
so long now,
death is just something
that happens.

To all of us.
And to me it's happening today.

>Pause.

MARK: My role is—
To make sure they do everything
properly.
PETER: Yes.

>*Long pause. Hold it for longer then the actors think they can.*

MARK: And so I—
Sorry—
PETER: —
MARK: Can you—?

>*Gesticulates to the scales.*

I need your correct weight—

>PETER *steps on the scales.*

>MARK *checks the scales and writes down the amount.*

Thank you, that's all the requirements
for now /
PETER: Does it feel strange?
Talking to me?
Knowing that in less than an
hour you'll see me dead?
MARK: —
PETER: How many times have you—?
MARK: No I haven't—
Never.
Not this.
PETER: But you've seen death up close?
MARK: —
PETER: What does it feel like to—
To see the life go?
MARK: —
PETER: Will it hurt?

>MARK *shakes his head.*

>*Pause.*

MARK: No.
PETER: They won't let my mother touch me.
MARK: I'm afraid that's the law here.
   It's— [cruel.]
PETER: Yes. But when you think about it,
in other places something
like that, like touch, it's not valued so much.
So in a weird way,
it's strangely human, isn't it?

   Beat.

   MARK *might slowly shrug, there is nothing to say to that.*

I'm not brave, you know.
She thinks I'm innocent,
my mother—

   Beat.

But I guess you never fucked up.

   Pause.

   MARK *goes to call for the guard.*

   MARK *stops and stares into* PETER*'s face.*

MARK: I held a heart in my hand,
a tiny new heart filled with potential,
held it until it stopped.
Before I went into the surgery that day
I looked the mother of that baby
in the eyes,
right into her eyes, like this,

   And he locks eyes with PETER.

and I said to her,
Trust me.
I told her to trust me with the life of
her warm, beautiful child.
Hand me your baby, I said.
No need for goodbyes.
No need for goodbyes.

Pause.

PETER: No need for goodbyes.

    A bell is rung outside.

MARK: I'm afraid,
    Peter, it's time.
    I will walk with you

        PETER *hesitates.*

PETER: Can you do something?
    Not for me,
    but my mum,
    if I hug you—?
    Can you give it to her?

MARK: I can't—
    I'm sorry—
    The rules,
    it's not allowed.

    MARK *physically backs off.*

PETER: I just thought that if—

    MARK *still can't do it, but emotionally he is there.*

MARK: Are you very frightened?

PETER: No.

MARK: —

PETER: —

MARK: —

PETER: Yes.

    MARK *stares at him*

    The bell rings again.

SCENE 25

AREZU *sits there alone.*
There is airport noise but no-one else is around now.
Her phone rings.
She picks up her phone and looks at it.

AREZU: Hello, Mum?
Mum?

> *She listens for a while.*
> *She stares straight ahead.*

I know.
It's okay, Maman.

> *A tear.*
> *(Her mother has said, 'I love you'.)*

You too, Maman, you too.

> *She hangs up the phone.*
> *Silence.*

> *She feels in her bag. Finds her hijab and puts it on.*
> *She sits a moment.*
> *Then she gets up, takes her bag, gets out her passport and papers. Heads toward the gate or check-in desk for her flight.*

> AREZU *leaves.*

> SASKIA *remains, in her space.*

SCENE 26

Can be spoken by any actor or surtitled, maybe both in this instance:
> 'We forget that human touch is life-giving.
> We do not remember that for millions of years we have received comfort, support, warmth and compassion through touch.'

ALICE *is clutching a photograph of her son.*
MARK *sits opposite her.*
There is silence for a long time.
MARK *is watching her in her resigned, vacant grief.*
Perhaps the actor playing PETER *stands in the background.*

MARK: Your son

She looks up at him.

Peter.
He gave me something to give you.

—

Something
from him.

ALICE: —?

> MARK *stands up and walks over to her.*
>
> ALICE *stands up.*
>
> MARK *is tentative, takes his time, then raises his arms and engulfs her carefully and tentatively into a hug.*
>
> *She recognises that it is a hug from her dead son and collapses into it, clinging to* MARK *as if he is her son.*
>
> *After some time* MARK *loosens into the hug himself, and at a certain stage closes his eyes and participates in the feeling of a person.*
>
> *Perhaps he finally rests his head on her shoulder; perhaps he has silent tears falling on the back of this childless mother.*
>
> *She will not let go.*
>
> *And neither will he.*

THE END

www.ingramcontent.com/pod-product-compliance
Lightning Source LLC
Chambersburg PA
CBHW050821090426
42737CB00022B/3465